THE STOCK MARKET INVESTING GUIDE #2020

From Beginner to Intelligent Investor within 30 Days - How to Save Money, Generate Passive Income and Reach Financial Freedom incl. ETF Special

RICHARD G. SOROS

CONTENTS

STOCK MARKET

Stock market (securities market) – is a collectivity of members in a stock market and legal relations between them, concerning accommodation, turnover and securities accounting.

The stock market is divided into **primary** and **secondary.**

1. The primary stock market is a complex of law relations associated with securities placement. The secondary stock market is a complex of law relations related to bonds turnover.

Stock market major participants are:

■ **Issuers.** An issuer may be a legal person, natural person, state or local government. The issuer places securities on his behalf and is obliged to accomplish duties arising from the conditions of their issue. By exercising the right of the issue (granted on certain conditions), the issuer is obliged to grant rights enshrined with the issued securities to their owners. Issued securities include travelers' checks, stocks, bonds, credit cards.

The issue includes two main functions: the right to place securities and obligation to grant the rights, enshrined with issued securities. In some cases, the issuer delegates the right of securities placement to third parties but keeps the securities obligation by himself. In this case, a third party receives issued securities as a reward. Similar schemes are found in the issue of Euro cents and bitcoins.

■ **Securities investors** - individuals and entities, residents and non-residents, who have acquired a property right for securities in order to obtain income from invested funds or/and acquiring the corresponding rights that are granted to securities owner by legislation.

- **Institutional investors** are institutions of common investment (unit and corporate investment funds), investment funds, mutual funds investment companies, non-state pension funds, insurance companies, other financial institutions that transact financial assets according to interests of third parties at their own expense or the expense of these parties and, in cases envisaged by the government, also for the expense of other financial assets involved by the other parties to receive income or preserve a real cost of financial assets.

- **Self-regulatory organization** of professional stock market participants - is a non-profit association of stock-market participants providing professional business in a stock market concerning securities trading, asset management of institutional investors, depository activity (the activity of registrars and custodians) established according to criteria and requirements imposed by the National Securities and Stock Market Commission. Professional participants of a stock market - are legal entities who carry out the professional activity on the stock market on the basis of a license issued by the State Commission on Securities and Stock Market.

- **Broker-Dealers** - Broker-dealers charge a fee for working with transactions between buyers and sellers of securities.

- **Transfer Agents** - Transfer agents report changes in the security ownership, keep track of the issuer's security holder, revoke and issue licenses, and manage dividends. Transaction agents stay among issuing firms and security holders.

- **Credit Rating Agencies -** Credit rating agencies give recommendations on the creditworthiness or reliability of a product. Using a grade, they indicate the credit quality. Credit scores typically differentiate between an investment grade and a non-investment grade.

TRADING TOOLS IN THE STOCK MARKET

To get started in the stock market, an investor must select investment strategies and specific tools for working with them. It is important to have a distinct understanding of what opportunities each tool offers and what the risks are.

Stock market instruments can be divided into two main categories:

1. Securities (bonds, stocks, investment certificates, promissory notes)

2. Derivatives (futures, options).

Bond - is a kind of securities that confirms the presence of debt commitments of the issuer in relation to its owner. The bond is issued for a specified period, after which the company or state that issued the security must pay the holder a certain amount that exceeds the initial acquisition costs.

Stock - is security confirming the fact of the participation of the owner in the formation of the authorized capital of a company.

The stock is divided into **ordinary** and **preferred**.

■ **The ordinary stocks** – are the most widely-used financial tool in the stock exchange. It was trading in this type of securities for a long time that made up the bulk of transactions carried out in the stock market. Today, the number of transactions with bonds and derivatives has increased markedly, but the stocks are still the most traded assets on most stock exchanges. An important feature of the shares is their perpetual nature.

- **The preferred stocks** - provide an opportunity to receive a certain and pre-fixed income, but do not provide the right to participate in the management of a company or corporation for their holder.

Investment certificate - is a security that certifies the fact of investing money in an investment fund and the right to receive part of the fund's income. The investment fund is a wholesale investor that raises and accumulates the funds of its investors to optimize the investment management costs.

Promissory note - is a security that includes a deferral of payment or unconditional payment for the goods, works or services purchased in advance. It confirms the responsibility of an owner (drawer) to pay the mentioned sum of money to a creditor (noteholder) through the agreed term after the presentation of a promissory note for the payment.

Option - is an agreement according to which a prospective buyer or prospective seller obtains the right, but not the obligation, to buy or sell the asset at a pre-agreed price at a specified contractual moment in the future or for a specified period.

Futures - is a derivative financial instrument, a standard exchange contract for the purchase of a basic asset (index, stock), after which the parties agree only on the price level and the delivery time. Futures on the stock market index and shares of individual issuers may be traded on the forward market.

THE PRINCIPAL TYPES OF AGREEMENTS WITH SECURITIES

Derivatives are financial agreements, the cost of which depends on a basic asset or asset group. The most widespread assets are currencies, bonds, goods and market indexes stocks. The cost of the basic assets is permanently changed according to the market conditions. The main principle of signing the derivatives is receiving a profit through speculation on the basic asset cost in the short run. Imagine that the market price of the stock may increase or decrease. Then there is a risk of facing damages due to the falling of the stock cost. In this situation, you can conclude a derivative or make a profit by placing an accurate bet.

There are 4 main types of agreements with securities:

1. Forwards

2. Futures

3. Swaps

4. Options

Forwards resemble the futures agreements, where the owner is obliged to execute a contract. The forwards are non-standard and are not traded on the stock exchanges. Generally, they are available over-the-counter, are not marked-to-market and set according to meet demands of the parties of the contract.

Futures are structured contracts that require the buyer to purchase/sell the asset at the agreed price at the defined date. The parties to the proposed deal are responsible to execute the deal. These futures are being exchanged on the stock market. The value of future contracts is represented on the market every day. This means that the contract value is changed by the price fluctuations until the expiration date.

Swaps are the derivatives where two parties share their financial commitments. Cash flows are based on a conditional major sum of the underlying amount agreed between the parties without exchanging a basic cost. The amount of the cash flow is based on a percentage rate. As a rule, one cash flow is fixed and another one is changed on the basis of a benchmark percentage rate. The interest rate swaps are the most widely-used class. They are not sold on the stock exchanges and are over-the-counter agreements between businesses and financial institutions.

Options are the derivatives that entitle a buyer to buy or sell the basic asset at a defined price during a certain period. A purchaser doesn't carry any obligations to execute an option. A seller of the options is called an "option write". The specified price is known as a "strike price". You can exercise American options at any time before the expiry of the option period. However, European options can only be exercised on the expiry date.

HOW TO MAKE MONEY ON THE STOCK EXCHANGE FOR A BEGINNER?

It is quite real to earn money on the stock exchange for beginners. But it is worth realizing that trading is not a game. If you are a newbie and want to make real money on the stock exchange, it is necessary to study the art of trading, understand the laws of the market, figure out technical and fundamental analysis.

And even after mastering all the necessary skills, it will not be easy for many to make money on the stock exchange since for this type of activity, it is essential to have a certain mindset.

People, who strive to study and analyze the stock market seriously, will achieve a big success in the investment business.

For instance, you are willing to buy the McDonalds shares, but, before this acquisition, you should compare the indicators of the company with the other competitors in the field, maybe, there exists a small company but with bigger growth prospects. To grow 2 times bigger, McDonald's needs much more effort, than any other small company, which will be enough to open restaurants in a new city.

To cash in on the stock exchange, you should possess the following features:

■ The ability to analyze;

■ Perseverance;

■ Flair.

---

2 ways to earn money on the stock exchange:

1. Trading

2. Investment

There is no significant difference between trading and investing, it is too blurred.

Plenty of experts reach a consensus that trading is short-term and medium-term deals during the day or week, and investments imply a more long-term approach.

Another group of specialists believes that the investments are aimed more at a passive income (dividends), rather than the resale of an asset.

How much can the beginner earn on the stock exchange?

Doubts about whether it is realistic to make money on the exchange via the Internet are dispelled. However, what income can a novice trader expect?

Under favorable circumstances, the beginner investor can earn about 20-50% for the first year (experienced ones can make a profit in the region of 100% per annum or more).

The traders can earn a larger percentage of profits, but they have to spend more time on work. 1-3% per trading day can be considered as an excellent result.

However, several conditions must coincide:

- Permanent studying;

- Predisposition to trading;

- The presence of a strict discipline by following management-risk and analytics.

If you started from scratch, after reading the literature and practicing on small amounts in 5-10 transactions, then 0% and saved money is already quite fine. Since having no losses means you, at least, understand the market.

PROFESSIONAL ACTIVITY IN THE STOCK MARKET

Professional activity in the stock market is the activity of legal entities providing services in the area of placement and turnover of securities, accounting of the securities' rights, and asset management of institutional investors in the stock market that conforms to the established requirements.

According to the law, it is not allowed to combine professional activity in the stock market with any other kinds of professional activity except for banking. It is also not allowed to combine certain types of professional activity in the stock market, except in cases provided by law.

The prerequisites for conducting professional activity in the stock market are:

☑ The presence of a license issued by the State Commission on Securities and Stock Market;

☑ Membership of at least one self-regulatory organization.

The following kinds of professional activity are carried out in the stock market:

1. Trading in securities;

2. Asset management of institutional investors;

3. The depository activity;

4. Organizing the stock market trading.

Trading in securities on the stock market is conducted by securities traders – business associations, for which securities transactions are exclusive activities, and also by banks.

The professional trading securities activity includes:

- Brokerage;

- Dealer activity;

- Underwriting;

- Securities management activity.

It is worth mentioning that the prerequisite for conducting such kinds of activity is the presence of an appropriate share capital amount. The securities trader can carry out the dealer activity if he has paid-up share capital of at least $20 000, a brokerage of at least 1 million, an underwriting or securities management activity of not less than 7 million. Besides, the share capital of another securities trader may not exceed 10%.

Apart from that, the securities trader is forbidden to resell and exchange his issued securities.

Brokerage activity – signing of civil law contracts (including commission agreements, proxies) by the securities trader concerning bonds on his behalf (on another party's behalf), by a proxy and at the expense of another person.

Dealer activity - signing of civil law contracts by the securities trader concerning bonds on his behalf and at his expense for resale.

Underwriting - securities placement (signing, selling) by the securities trader by a proxy on his behalf and at the expense of an issuer.

In case of public placement of the securities, an underwriter may take over the obligation by an agreement with the issuer regarding a sell guarantee of all issuer's securities that are liable to placement or their parts. If the issue of securities is publically placed (but not fully),the underwriter may commit a full or partial redemption of non-realized securities for a fixed price based on a commercial representation according to his commitments.

To achieve a more efficient organization of the public placement of the securities, the underwriters may agree on joint activities.

The securities management activity – is the activity that is conducted by the securities trader on his behalf for the reward during a definite term. It is carried out on the ground of a management agreement in the form of securities and financial resources that are intended for investment in the securities.

The management agreements may be signed by both individuals and legal entities. An important prerequisite is that the amount of the securities management agreement with one client - an individual, must be at least the amount equivalent to 100 minimum wages.

The securities trader might act as a bail bondsman or guarantor of compliance with the obligations in front of third parties under contracts, concluded on a client's behalf of such trader, receiving the reward for this, determined by the securities trader contract with the client.

The contract of an agency, commissions or the securities management agreement is concluded with the securities trader in a written form. Such agreement envisages:

☑ Rights and duties of the securities trader concerning his client;

☑ The terms of concluding the securities agreements;

☑ Accounting treatment of the trader in front of his client;

☑ The procedure and terms of a reward payment to the trader.

The securities trader is obliged to execute the clients' orders under the concluded contracts on the most favorable terms for the client.

The securities trader keeps a record of all bonds and financial resources separately from each client and separately from securities, financial resources and property that are in his possession.

The securities trader is obliged to submit to the stock exchange of his choice, information about all transactions performed by him with securities in time and, according to the order, specified by the rules of the stock exchange.

The securities' trading that is not regarded as a professional activity:

■ The placement of own securities by the issuer;

■ The redemption of own securities by the issuer;

■ Making calculations using promissory notes and/or mortgages by individuals and legal entities-entrepreneurs;

■ Deposit of securities in the authorized capital of legal entities.

The following transactions may be conducted without the securities trader:

❑ Donation and inheritance of securities;

❑ Transactions associated with the court decision;

❑ Share acquisition according to the Law of Privatization.

1. **Asset management of institutional investors** is the professional activity of a stock market participant - asset Management Company that is conducted by it as a reward on its behalf or the ground of an appropriate contract concerning the asset management of institutional investors.

2. **Depository activity** is a complex of actions including providing services, regarding the storage of securities regardless of an issue form, opening and maintaining accounts in securities, providing transaction service in these accounts (including clearing and securities settlements under the contracts) and service of issuer's transactions concerning issued by his securities.

3. **Organizing stock market trading** is an activity of a professional stock market participant (trade organizer) in creating organizational, technological, informational, legal and other conditions for collection and dissemination of information regarding supply and demand. Also, a regular solicitation process with financial instruments according to the established rules.

The clearing is the conduct of transactions by the cashless settlement based on a mutual set-off of obligations. Basically, the clearing is formalized between states.

A BROKERAGE ACCOUNT

A brokerage account is a personal «pocket» for the storage of financial resources and securities that is opened by a licensed company broker. It is necessary for conducting such transactions as buying and selling stocks, bonds, currency, and any other financial instruments nationwide and on the international marketplace.

How does it work?

The brokerage account is as follows. A client visits a company (to broker) and formalizes an agreement about the opening of the account. After that, he deposits funds on a balance and, with the assistance of a special program or app, manages the money.

When there is a need for buying stocks, bonds or currency, the client generates an appropriate request via program, app or cell phone. The broker confirms the deal, and, after that, the sum of investments and the broker's commission are withdrawn from the account. Then the client is given a record at his account that he has become an owner of the bought financial assets.

According to a collaboration form and type of transactions, we can distinguish the following types of the brokerage accounts:

- **A cash account** – is the simplest and the most popular one because you can make investible transactions instantly after the registration and depositing the funds.

- **An individual account** has some restrictions. It is not allowed to close the account and move money out earlier than in 3 years after opening it.

- **A margin account** – when the broker provides additional services for the client, including the credit funds for trade in the stock market.

- **An option account** - there appears an opportunity to trade options. An option is an agreement to buy or sell an underlying asset (for example stocks, or ETF) at a definite price within a specified timeframe. Although the options potentially could help you to protect your portfolio, generate income or speculate on the market, some risks should be taken into consideration. Approval is required before you can take advantage of this account feature.

- **A joint account** - this account is divided between 2 or more individuals. The joint brokerage accounts are frequently conducted by spouses but are also opened by the family members such as a father and a child or by 2 individuals who have common financial goals (for example, business partners).

Advantages of a brokerage account for an ordinary person

Nowadays, more and more people are interested in the opening of the brokerage account. Standard bank investments, despite their safety, don't generate enough income for investors.

So, we might single out the following underlying pros of the brokerage account:

☑ The opportunity of buying securities and stocks of such international corporations like Google, Amazon, Facebook, etc. After the investment, a person can get dividends and regular passive income, and also the possibility of earning on increasing the value of stocks.

☑ The brokerage account is an alternative to bank deposits. The average annual rate in a financial organization only slightly covers an inflation rate. It is important to realize that the world's political situation, financial performance and the compliance of the outcome of the activity to analysts' expectations influence a rate of returns.

☑ High asset liquidity as an opportunity to sell the asset quickly.

☑ It is the source of additional income. Companies pay out dividends to their investors regardless of the financial outcomes. When a lot of stocks are accumulated, the dividends provide a stable passive income.

What is the best way to cash in on the brokerage account?

The earnings in the securities and stocks require having certain knowledge and skills. Otherwise, the investment will be more like a gambler's game than a balanced investible approach. The main ways to earn in the securities are:

☑ Receiving dividends - companies distribute net profit, obtained according to the outcomes of a reporting period between the shareholders. The payment size is changed by an organization's financial success.

☑ Making money on the growth – buying stocks at a low cost and selling after a while at a much higher price.

☑ Making money on reduction – buying stocks in debt from a broker in order to redeem them in case of stock dips. Then, the borrowed money is brought back out of the obtained income.

Pitfalls a newbie should be aware of:

Broker's services are advertised on every street corner, saying it is possible to earn big money in the short term. In most cases, advertisers use images of successful people who generate income quickly and easily. But, usually, companies hide and keep silent about potential loss. The following examples will help you to be acquainted with the most common broker's pitfalls:

- A long-term investment - financial experts reach a consensus that, with a high probability, you can earn money only having created a diversified long-term portfolio for securities.

- Brokers cash in on commission – companies stimulate people to fulfill dozens of agreements to receive income for service.

- Technical analysis - an instrument that helps to comprehend that the best way to make a contract and back out of it is to keep track of the market tendencies rather than predict the following cost movement.

- Paid analytics – brokers perform analytical services for an additional payment to help clients to choose an asset for buying.

- Frauds can pretend to be brokers on their networking sites and offer an opening of the brokerage account, though they are not related to brokerage activity at all. They are involved in this field with the sole goal -to rip you off.

HOW TO OPEN A BROKERAGE ACCOUNT? STEP-BY-STEP GUIDE.

Choosing the right brokerage account may seem a complicated process at a first glance. Firstly, you should figure out what type of account you want to open and then, comparing several online stock brokers, you will be able to choose the one that fits your demands.

Here are your step-by-step instructions on opening the brokerage account:

- Identify the type of the brokerage account you need;

- Compare incentives and costs;

- Consider the suggested services and facilities;

- Solve on a brokerage company;

- Top up the account;

- Fill out a new account application;

- Kick off researching investments.

1. Identify the type of brokerage account you need

What are your investible objectives? If you just plan to invest funds for a rainy day or a near-term goal and you have no desire to tie your money up before retirement, open a traditional brokerage account. These accounts don't have tax advantages but the tax on investment profits and dividends may have to be paid. Besides, you are free and able to withdraw money whenever you want.

If you set your sights on a cash account, your broker will question you if you long for margin privileges. It means you can borrow money on buying stocks. In doing so, your stocks will serve as collateral. You will pay out interest on the borrowed money. Also, there exist some inherent risks connected to the margin investment you should be aware of.

On the other hand, if your goal is to set on saving your money for a future pension, IRA is the best bet. The conventional IRAs can receive tax deductions when you contribute to them, although you won't have an opportunity to utilize the money until the age of 59-1/2.

In fact, contributions to the Roth IRAs don't provide you tax concessions when you contribute them, but qualified withdrawals will be tax-free. Besides, you may withdraw the contributions anytime you want. At the end of the day, if you are self-employed, there are some particular options such as SIMPLE IRA, SEP-IRA, or individual 401(k).

2. Compare incentives and costs

For the time being, there is a bunch of discount brokers who come up with the commission-free trading. Usually, they offer a discount in order to provoke performing certain actions like trading at a high volume or maintaining a savings account in the same company.

Consequently, it is extremely important to look through the brokers' full pricing schedule, particularly if you make plans with trading options, funds, bonds, anything except stocks. For instance, the majority of brokers charge 0, 80 per options contract over their standard commission rate.

Also, a lot of brokers recommend incentives to drum up and attract business, and you don't need to be a millionaire to take advantage of them.

3. Consider the suggested services and facilities

Pricing is not everything, particularly for new investors. Certainly, it is much better to find the lowest price at all other equal things, but some other things need to be taken into account when choosing the broker:

❏ Researching access – many brokers grant their stock ratings and access to third-party research from firms like Standard & Poor's and Morningstar.

❏ Trading abroad - some brokers come up with the opportunity to convert money from your account in a foreign currency with a view to trading on the international marketplace. If it takes precedence for you, then make sure that the chosen broker allows this.

❏ Trading platforms - varied brokerage services offer a wide range of trading software and mobile apps. Actually, some of such brokerage services allow people to check their platforms before opening the account. For instance, Fidelity suggests a demo-version of its platform Active Trader Pro for their potential clients to test drive.

❏ Convenience - some brokerage companies have big networks of local branch offices. You might attend for your investment, while others – no. For instance, clients of Merrill Edge can receive some tips and recommendations eye-to-eye at more than 2,000 the Bank of America locations. Besides, the brokerage services that are ruled by banks, suggest clients an option to connect their checking and brokerage accounts, transferring money between the accounts in a real-time schedule.

They also may offer a certain «discount on relations» for doing so. It is also preferable to check if your bank has an online brokerage.

❏ Other side functions. This list is not comprehensive, so before choosing the broker, spend time on websites, analyzing and learning what he offers. Only in this way, you will be «prepared».

4. Solve on a brokerage company

You have collected all the whole information about expenses, fees and services they offer in different companies. You should weigh all for and against, which relate to your investment objectives, and determine which broker is suitable for you.

5. Fill out a new account application

You can apply for the opening of a new account on the Net. You will need to identify information. For instance, your Social Security number and your driver's license. Also, you are likely to sign some additional forms if you require margin privileges and/or a chance to sell options. By the way, the broker will need to collect information about your net income, employment status, investible assets and goals.

6. Top up the account

Your new broker will possibly give you several ways of transferring the money to your account. They could be:

■ **An asset transfer** - if you transfer existing investments from another broker or rollover 401(k), it is the most acceptable way of investment.

■ **A wire transfer** - the fastest way of financing your account. Although the wire transfer is a direct money transfer in a bank, it frequently happens within several minutes.

- **An electronic funds transfer** – the wire transfer with a connected savings or checking account. It is a convenient way of financing the account. In many cases, your funds will be posted on the account the next business day.

- **Checks** – acceptable forms of check deposits and the presence of funds differ amongst brokers.

- **Stock certificates**. Yes, that's true - they still exist. If you have a paper stock certificate, you may deposit it via mail into the brokerage account.

In conclusion, when you fund your brand, bear in mind your broker's minimums. A lot of them have various minimums for taxable accounts, as well as pension accounts. They also could have sundry minimum requirements for margin accounts.

7. Kick off researching investments

Felicitations on taking the initiative and opening the brokerage account, you will be thankful to yourself for this important step on the way to financial safety.

Now, the most interesting part comes... The investment in stocks. Before diving, you will have to spend time learning the basics about how to choose stocks, bonds or financial resources properly and also how to create a well-diversified portfolio.

THE INTERACTION WITH A BROKER

If you decided to trade on the stock exchange, you have two ways. The first is to trust a manager. This method is suitable for those, who are short of time or do not have a desire to be engaged in investing on their own. The second option is to do everything by yourself: develop a strategy for investing money and take responsibility for transactions.

However, you can't come on the stock exchange and trade yourself. You will need to have a broker- an intermediary between an investor and an issuer, i.e. between you and a company, whose securities you are planning to buy. A broker is a company which has a license to work on the stock market and a right to make securities transactions for the investor.

How to interact with the broker?

1. **Enter into a contract with the broker**. Study the contract terms about the broker's service. As a rule, brokers publish the typical agreement with tariffs on their websites. If you are satisfied with the prices and other terms, you can draw a contract at a broker's office or send notarized documents by email.

2. **Set up a securities accoun**t. The securities you buy must be accounted for somewhere. Open a custody account in the depository (an account for securities). The depository may be a separate company that is not related to your broker. But frequently, in addition to the broker license, the broker has a depository and combines these two functions.

3. **Transfer money to the broker** to allow him to buy the securities for you. It is more beneficial to open

an individual investment account for accounting this money. It will help you save taxes.

4. Now, you are ready to trade on the exchange - you can **give errands to the broker**: to buy and sell the securities. This can be done by phone, online, using a special program - a trading terminal, or through a broker's mobile application.

5. The broker, on your behalf, **carries out the transactions in the stock market**. In addition to the money purchased from the securities, a commission is withdrawn from the brokerage account - a fee for the broker assisting you to cope with these operations.

6. With the help of the broker, you can **withdraw the money** to your bank account (which can also include some commission). The broker will **calculate and withhold the tax** on your income.

How to choose the broker? Evaluation of potential risks.

You should bear in mind that the funds on your brokerage account don't get into the deposit insurance system, unlike the bank deposits. Therefore, your task is to find the most reliable broker.

Here are the things you must check before choosing the broker:

■ **A license**. First and foremost, check (The Bank Credit Analysis Handbook), if the broker has the license of a professional participant of the stock market securities. If no - he is a fraud. Make sure that the name of the company in the register correlates with the one broker mentions in the contract. It may turn out that the broker offers you to sign the agreement with a "partner" foreign company that has a very similar name. If you sign the agreement with the foreign broker and he violates your rights, you will have to defend your interests in the country where he is registered.

- **Financial indicators**. Check out the list of the largest brokers. The large volumes of trading do not guarantee complete peace of mind. However, it means the company has many customers, who trust it with significant capital.

- **Reputation**. Explore the broker's website and read the customers' feedbacks on the Internet. Pay attention to the history of the company - whether its name was involved in financial conflicts. Look for financial news – suddenly, you can discover something interesting about the potential broker.

- **Risks**. Before signing the contract with the broker, read a risk notice. This document describes why you could lose money by trading in the securities market in a detailed way.

- **Terms**. Study the conditions of the brokerage services carefully. Pay attention to these details: commissions, terms of money transfer, interest on loans – in case you plan to buy securities with the broker's expenses. Find out if the broker can use your money and securities for personal interests and how much the commission will grow if you forbid him to do so.

THE COLLECTION OF THE GREATEST ONLINE BROKERS 2020

If you are going to buy shares of stocks such as Facebook, Apple, UBER or DIS, then you will need an online brokerage account.

The most important decision that you make as an investor is choosing an online stockbroker.

The best online brokers 2020:

- E*TRADE – The best web platform

- TD Ameritrade – Best for professionals and beginners

- Trade Station – The best platform technology

- Interactive Brokers – Best for professionals

- Charles Schwab – Best for IRA accounts

- Merrill Edge – The best rewards program

- Fidelity – The best research experience

E * TRADE was established in 1982 as one of the first online-brokers in the USA. It knows what investors need to reach success on the market. E*TRADE includes $0 stock trades, Power E*TRADE platform, which is perfectly suitable for options trading, and two amazing mobile apps.

Why is **E * TRADE** widely chosen?

- An excellent web-platform that is the winner in options trading. It is ease at use and has fantastic trading tools.

- Multifunctional mobile apps. E * TRADE, among all online brokers, offers lots of well-created mobile app functions.

TD Ameritrade provides a full package for investors including $0 trades, excellent marketing research, leading education for beginners, fantastic trading platforms and reliable customer service. This all-round and outstanding experience makes TD Ameritrade the top broker of 2020.

Why **TD Ameritrade** is widely chosen?

- Reliable research. TD Ameritrade gives the customers access to its TV Network and trader shop. In addition, TD Ameritrade also uses own data to analyze millions of tweets to use its tool - Social Signals.

- Perfectly suitable for newbie investors. TD Ameritrade has the biggest choice of educational materials. By far, this branch has more than 200 training videos highlighting any investment topic. Moreover, the whole educational center is gamified, keeping track of your progress during the quiz time, bringing the concept together at the end of each course.

- Industry-leading technology. TD Ameritrade is the only broker that offers clients an opportunity to get access to their accounts on Twitter, Alexa, Apple Chat and Facebook. Innovations and latest technologies are core parts of the TD Ameritrade's DNA.

TradeStation supports random traders via its web-based platform and active traders through its award-winning desktop platform, all with a $0 stock and ETF trades.

Why **TradeStation** is widely chosen?

- Wonderful mobile app for stocks and options trading. TradeStation Mobile provides an unforgettable experience in the entire world. It monitors multiple watch lists, sets price notifications, and analyzes the stock charts and trading places.

- The best trading platform. TradeStation 10 is a desktop trading platform for downloading conducted online. It is full of robust trading tools.

Interactive Brokers is a branch of low-price trading for professionals. Interactive Brokers offers high-quality tools and a wide variety of the securities traded.

Why **Interactive Brokers** is widely chosen?

- Global access. Interactive Brokers offers trading in 27 countries and more than 126 market outlets. It is the most diverse offer by a landslide.

- Perfectly suitable for daily trading. Interactive Brokers doesn't accept payment for order flow (IBKR Pro only). It makes its low prices look much better as there are no hidden execution expenses.

- The best choice for professional traders. Margin rates are the lowest in the industry. Moreover, Interactive Brokers suggest its clients more than 60 different order types.

Charles Schwab is a brokerage with a wide range of services. It was founded in 1973 and has more than $3 trillion of total clients' assets. Being a leader of a low-cost policy, Charles Schwab offers $0 stock trades, high-quality trade tools, professional future planning, and superb stock research.

Why **Charles Schwab** is widely chosen?

- The leader in retirement services. This broker glitters with its smart portfolios Schwab and Schwab Intelligent Portfolios Premium services.

- Perfect market research. It may boast of its lineup from 26 inside experts who perform plenty of various articles on diverse market topics during the whole week.

Merrill Edge trades with ETF – a wonderful research and client's service. Apart from that, it delivers $0 stocks by supporting a parent company Bank of America. Furthermore, there is a program, «Preferred Rewards», that provides the best reward advantages for the present banking customers.

Why **Merrill Edge** is widely chosen?

- Fantastic research ESG (management, ecology and social sphere). Merrill Edge offers stocks like Portfolio Story, Story and Fund Story. As a result, it makes the conducting of market research both insightful and educational.

- Reward advantage. If you want to open an account in Merrill Edge, there is no need to be a customer of the Bank of America. In fact, it is much easier to reach a minimal combined account balance to gain all kinds of perks within the Preferred Rewards program.

- Upscale customer service. Having made national testing, it was discovered that Merrill Edge consistently delivered agent connection times under one minute.

Fidelity is a value-oriented broker offering industry-advanced research, $0 stock trades, and high-quality trade tools. Moreover, it has a good mobile app and offers comprehensive retirement services. It is the leader of everyday investors by serving more than 30 million customers.

Why **Fidelity** is widely chosen?

■ Finest mobile app for everyday investors. The Fidelity mobile app is the winner among investors because it is simple, includes plenty of trade tools and is fully-packed with market researches.

■ Wonderful for investible research. The research of the Fidelity company stands out with their 17 research reports, perfect inside market analysis and quotes of the experience.

■ Perfectly suitable for new investors. Fidelity offers an ideal mixture of easy usability for investors, a nice educational center and superb research tools. Fidelity is the second broker advice for newbie stock traders according to TD Ameritrade.

ACQUISITION OF YOUR FIRST STOCKS

You have decided to make investments in the stock market and even have some views on which stocks you want to buy. So, what is the best way to buy stocks?

Fortunately, the buying process of your first stocks is relatively simple and quick.

Here is a **step-by-step guide for making your first investment.**

1. Find the best online broker for you (read our special chapter about it)

2. Open and commence financing your brokerage account

3. Decide which stocks you want to buy

4. Make up a decision on how many stocks to buy

5. Select the order type

6. Enter your stock orders

7. Lean back in the chair and chill out

1. Find the best online broker for you

There are two main things you should think of while comparing online brokers: if your broker fits your demands and if its trade platform is simple to use.

- Is the platform user-friendly and easily navigated? If you are going to trade via your cell phone or any other mobile device, you must make sure that the mobile broker's platform is convenient for you. Fortunately, a lot of famous brokers tend to test out their trade platform with playing money before you register. Try several and select the best one.

■ Does your broker offer everything you need? For instance, some brokers offer excellent educational resources for newbie investors, useful high-quality tools, access to stocks research, and others. Some of them offer personal offices so that if you make up your mind to receive an eye-to-eye guidance, it might be just a short drive. Other features, which can be relevant, include the trade opportunity in the international stock market and the possibility to buy fractional shares of stocks.

2. Open and fund your account

The next step after choosing a broker is filling out the application in the account. It is compulsory to have a driver's license, the bank account information, and the Social Security number if you are going to top up your new account from savings or check the account. As a rule, it is a fast process. When you fill out an application in the account, you ought to consider 2 things:

■ Do you want options for the trade benefits? If you are a newbie investor, it would be a great idea to keep off from options until you find out what you are doing. There exist several privilege levels to choose from.

■ Do you want the margin benefits? It means you will have a chance to borrow money for buying stocks. However, the margin investment is not a good idea. On the other hand, the presence of margin privileges may be useful in some cases.

---

3. Decide which stocks you want to buy

Another step is stock identification.

■ Focus on a long-term prospect. Before buying stocks – think rationally. Buy the ones you would like to own for years, not just for several weeks or months.

■ Diversification is also a smart decision. Don't deposit all your money in one or two stocks. Even if you kick off your account with a relatively low sum of money. It has become more practical to buy just a few shares of several various stocks with no trading commission.

4. Make up a decision of how many stocks to buy

A very first step if you want to define how many stocks you want to buy is determining how much money you want to invest in each stock. After that, divide this sum of money into a current stock price by either launching the search of the company on the brokerage platform or entering the stock's ticker symbol.

If your broker allows you to buy fractional shares, you can take advantage of this calculation. Most brokers don't allow this, so, you will need to round down to the nearest whole figure to determine how many stocks you want to buy.

5. Select the order type

You will find different order types. As a rule, market orders are the best for long-term investors.

Another common order type is known as a restriction. It let the broker know the maximum price you are ready to pay. For instance, if the stock you are planning to buy is traded for $20-50 per stock, but you want to buy it $20 less - you can establish a limited order.

Since you filled out your trading ticket and pressed the button «place order», it will take a matter of seconds before your broker accomplishes the order, and the shares show up on your account balance.

6. Enter your stock orders

The last step is to place the order with your broker. Here, you are going to enter a necessary stock symbol and/or how many stocks you thirst for.

7. Lean back in the chair and chill out

Having bought your first stocks, you can put your feet up and let the long-term stock market to do its work. If you want your dividends to be automatically reinvested in a bigger stock amount, you may enroll in the dividends reinvestment plan of your broker by pressing 1 button.

However, checking your stocks every day might sound tempting (particularly for the first time). But it is important to keep a long-term mindset.

Undoubtedly, you must keep up with the latest news about your company by reading quarterly reports. Even if your stocks go down, don't panic and sell. And otherwise, when your stocks go up, resist the temptation to withdraw cash. The best way to accumulate money over time is to buy large companies stocks and hang onto them until the right moment.

A NECESSITY OF INVESTMENT IN STOCKS

Any investments constitute an intensive activity in the finance field. Furthermore, any investments reflect the most important life principles of any adequate person. To live a better life in the short run, you should do your best right now.

There is an immense amount of investment tools. Some of them allow earning on short-term periods, while the others – in long-term prospects. Stocks are supposed to be investment tools working for the future. And if you want to sort out this investible procedure – get to know with its term.

Stocks are the securities that confirm their owners' rights on some assets of the company-issuer as well as the income part in the form of dividends.

The sale of stocks is conducted through the stock exchange. However, an individual doesn't have a right to make deals by himself in this market. This procedure must be carried out through intermediaries who act in the capacity of brokerage companies.

The right on the transactions with securities is given to the brokers on the ground of an issued license. To invest in stocks, you need to have a certain level of financial knowledge. Such awareness will help you to choose tools for purchase as it is quite silly to rely on your intuition.

It is worth knowing that there are no assurances under these investments. It is just impossible to predict where the stock price is likely to move in the short run.

However, there are no restrictions over the amounts of profitability under these investments. The stock cost may grow in a year on 100% and even 1000%, but there are also some situations when the stock price goes down significantly.

For those who wish to make money in the fastest way, investment in stocks is not the best choice. In this situation, you will need to look for tools with more short-term paybacks. Stocks will be suitable for people who set more long-term goals.

Stocks, which are generated on the stock exchange, are quite diverse. They differ according to a profitability level, a stock rate, and some other factors. Each investor selects securities according to personal strategy:

■ Some people decide to invest money in stocks of leading companies, such-called «blue chips»;

■ Other people consider investing their capital into new developing organizations.

Telling the truth, buying such stocks results in making a fortune. That's because investing your capital in the securities of production companies is similar to the real investment.

The most important stock characteristics and advantages.

Characteristics	Description
Unlimited profitability	The stocks' price grows in proportion to the growth of the assets' cost. Accordingly, when the organization actively develops, the price of its securities goes up.

Characteristics	Description
Diversity	There is a bunch of the assets of different companies for the investor to choose from.
High-liquidity level	Many shares are easily exchanged for money any day the stock market is opened.
Credibility	Stocks are legitimate financial tools under state protection.
The level of initial investments	You need a small amount of initial investment to start investing in stocks.

There are 2 main ways to cash in on the investments:

1. Receiving dividends is the simplest and most understandable way. In this case, a capital owner just acquires stocks and receives the part of the net income of the issuer-company. However, this choice is not always forward-looking and long-term.

2. Stock speculations can bring a much bigger profit rather than dividends payments. The basic principle of making a profit here is: to buy securities at a lower price ↓ and sell them at a higher price ↑. Consequently, for the sake of maximum profitability, you will have to study the stock market, analyze the situation, and make sound forecasts for the further movement of the course.

Since in most cases stock deals are made through brokers, it is essential to understand how such companies operate. Besides, the right choice of the intermediary is also significant.

ADVANTAGES AND DISADVANTAGES OF INVESTING IN STOCKS

Before deciding to invest in stocks, it is necessary to think about the advantages and disadvantages of this investment option. This approach helps to understand if this method of generating income is appropriate for a particular investor.

☑ Advantages

Firstly, let's consider possible advantages for the investor:

1. **A low initial investment.** In most cases, stock purchases can be made even if there is a small amount to invest;

2. **Trading on the stock exchange is available to almost all the investors.** Thanks to modern technologies, you can buy stocks without leaving home, through the services of the broker;

3. **The stock market is not a casino.** Provided that they have knowledge of the principles of operation of financial exchanges, it is possible to carry out speculative transactions with shares with high accuracy;

4. **The opportunity to receive 2 types of income at once** – in the form of dividends, as well as from speculative transactions;

5. **Large investors can influence the further direction of the issuer's development** in a favorable side by buying a block of shares of the company, thus receiving the right to participate in the shareholders' meetings;

6. **A high-liquidity level.** The shares of the largest issuers, which relate to the blue chips, have almost absolute liquidity, i.e. they can be sold quickly enough any time the investor wishes;

7. **Experience is not necessary at all**. By its absence, there is no need to refuse to invest in stocks, you can use the options to buy the units of the investment funds, as well as transfer funds to trust management;

8. **Unlimited profitability.** Selecting the right strategy, the size of the profit is not limited as you can make good money for the acquisition of shares after their short-term decline, along with the purchasing the securities of some developing organizations;

9. There is an opportunity to use the stock acquisition as both active and passive investments according to preferences of the owner of the capital;

10. In most cases, stock speculation is less risky than trading Forex instruments, as leverage is set at low or nonexistent risk when dealing with these securities.

☑ Disadvantages

We may single out the following disadvantages of investing in stocks:

1. **A high loss risk**. For example, when you invest the capital in the shares of one company or one industry. To reduce it, an investment portfolio will have to be formed which is quite difficult. In the absence of sufficient knowledge and experience of stock speculation, such activities are threatened by monetary losses. In addition, in case of the bankruptcy of the issuer, there is a likelihood of losing the invested capital completely.

2. **An adverse effect of the economic crisis.** If the investor makes a decision to deal with stocks that are not generated on the stock exchange, there is a high risk of a significant drop in liquidity during the crisis periods. The value of most stocks is also cheaper. In this case, the decline in the rate may be rapid, and its recovery – too slow.

3. **Additional expenses.** These include payments for the services of the brokerage, depository, and other companies, as well as operating and others.

4. **In the case of buying a little block of shares**, an investor can't influence The issuer's development and make decisions connected to the profit distribution as well.

5. **The unpredictability of the stocks' prices**. Plenty of factors influence their changes in cost, including political and economic ones (which are difficult to predict).

6. **The shareholders may end up with no dividends if the issuer**, after the end of the year, operates at a loss or decides to direct profits to the development of the company rather than the payments to the shareholders.

7. **Buying a stock is a long-term investment.** If it is too early to withdraw the capital, you may lose your planned profit, or even lose the whole profit.

THE MAIN WAYS OF INVESTING IN STOCKS

Deciding to invest in stocks, newcomers face the problem of choosing how to buy such securities. It is vital to know not only the available options but also the pros and cons of each way.

The 1st way. Purchase directly from the issuer

If the issuer offers this opportunity, you can buy the shares directly from the company that issued them. In most cases, direct investment is available for small and start-up companies.

Understand the sequence of actions required:

1. The investor visits an official website of the company assets of which he wants to buy. Here, you need to find the point where the information for the investors is placed.

2. The investing conditions should be carefully considered, the possible options must be analyzed and the investment returns need to be calculated. It is of great importance to study the contract carefully, determine the method and the procedure of receiving dividends, as well as find out the minimum possible amount of the investments.

3. If the investor is satisfied with all the points of the offer, it is necessary to register and send an application for the purchase of securities to the issuer. As a result, a company representative will contact the potential investor and inform you about the decision. Only after receiving the approval you can pay cash into the purchased shares.

If there is a desire to make direct investments, choose only large well-known companies with an impeccable reputation. In addition, the investor must be versed in the industry.

You should not buy stocks directly from the issuers for a large enough amount, as the risk is quite high.

The 2nd way. Acquisition of shares through the stock exchange

To make the investments as effective as possible, the broker should be chosen responsibly. Only when you are convinced that a reliable company has been selected for the cooperation, you can sign the agreement on the provision of intermediary services. After the transaction is completed, the investor opens an investment account.

There are several basic things you need to be aware of:

■ While performing the transaction, you will have to pay a commission, which, in most cases, is a few tenths of a percent of the transaction amount;

■ The broker does not make the decision on his own - he is only required to execute exactly the orders for the purchase of shares the investor gives him;

■ Large brokers offer a large number of favorable rates to the investor; there are the programs designed for the beginners;

■ The brokerage companies provide their clients with expert assistance – analytics reports and professional pieces of advice on what stocks to invest in this month;

- Newbie investors receive the opportunity to open demo accounts allowing them to try their hand at stock trading without investing big money.

When deciding to trade stocks on the stock exchange, first and foremost - study the functionality of the trading terminal and the sites carefully, analyze all the opportunities provided, understand how to raise capital.

The 3d way. The acquisition of investment fund units

Mutual investment fund constitutes a pool of the investor funds managed by the professionals, including MIF that earns on equity investments.

Such investments are passive earnings. The fund of a participant is not engaged in buying and selling shares, its income is determined only by the success of Mutual investment fund.

There are plenty of benefits the investor can get after investing in mutual funds:

- ☑ There is no need in taking actions except the purchase of shares;

- ☑ No big amount of money will be needed to start investing;

- ☑ The risk of investing is lower than that of buying shares independently, as the activity of the fund is controlled by the state and the depositary, as well as through regular audits of auditors;

- ☑ The assets of the shareholders are protected in case of bankruptcy of the fund. If this happens, the money will be transferred to another mutual fund.

Although investing in Mutual investment funds entails additional costs, including an account maintenance fee, this option is great for beginner investors. In case of the absence of any experience and sufficient knowledge of the stock exchange, investing directly in stocks is quite risky.

INVESTMENTS IN STOCKS.
INSTRUCTION FOR BEGINNERS.

Before start exploring the algorithm of investing capital in stocks, it is necessary to realize only free cash can be invested. Abandoning it for a long time should not affect the welfare and living standards of the investor.

The invested capital shouldn't consist of the money for some obligatory expenses.

Depending on the way of investing in stock the investor chooses, it is essential to stick to a certain algorithm.

The steps below are described in a detailed way and should be taken into account to make such investments.

1. Studying the stock market

Investments in stocks could cause serious damages without learning all ins and outs of this process.

A smarter way - is to figure out the basics of the stock market system. You should understand why stocks go up or down, why brokerage companies are necessary, and how to make a profit.

Then the question arises: where to look for the needed information? First of all, there is a lot to read, for example, specialized literature, as well as experts' articles.

However, there is no point in exploring all the information you see. Only credible sources and analytical articles written by experts should be taken into account.

The most useful books, where information is presented simply and understandably, are:

- "Rich Dad Poor Dad" by Robert T.Kiyosaki

- "The Essays of Warren Buffett"

- "Security Analysis" by Benjamin Graham

- "The Intelligent Investor" by Benjamin Graham

- "Common Stocks and Uncommon Profits" by Philip Fisher

Studying theoretical materials helps newcomers make predictions. This allows you to predict in which direction the stock price is likely to move.

2. The analysis of possible options

Even without financial education and hard sciences knowledge, you can invest in stocks. If there are enough desire and time, then you have all the chances to understand how different financial tools work.

Many people believe investing in financial resources in stocks to generate income requires huge investments like several million. But it is a misconception.

Initially, you can invest a small sum of money. Some brokers allow their clients to open their accounts by funding only $50 or $100. When it becomes clear that you can make money on a small number of investments, you can increase your working capital.

Another important tip for beginners is that you should not invest all your money in one company stock. The diversification of the investments is greatly important.

Ideally, the capital should be divided into 5 parts, which are distributed between the securities of different issuers. It is desirable for companies to work in different industries and to have maximum profitability in all the areas.

3. Predictability and choice

As we have already said, you must make predictions to guess in which direction the stock price is likely to move. It is not always possible for newbies to gain maximum accuracy.

If you have no time and desire to do your own analysis, you can use the ready-made predictions by experienced analysts. One more option – to ask a consultant for assistance. Such specialists always prompt which stocks acquisition will be more effective at a certain moment and vice versa.

Experts advise the beginners to practice trading stocks in a virtual account. Many brokers have the opportunity to open demo accounts allowing them to transact with securities without investing real money.

However, keep in mind that the virtual account is only a good choice for mastering the technical component of the issue. Psychologically, trading in demos and in real accounts are significantly different. When dealing with real money, the investor could face difficulties in coping with his emotions.

4. Stock acquisition

You will need to use the services of the brokerage company to buy shares on the stock exchange. Therefore, choosing a really reliable intermediary is essential.

Give preferences to the brokers that have:

- A license;

- Registration in your country.

If you open the account with the broker registered in another country, in case of problems, the money will have to be returned in accordance with the laws of that state. This process might turn out to be quite difficult.

When the brokerage account is opened and the money is deposited into it, you can order the broker to buy a certain number of shares of a particular company. All subsequent actions are determined according to the chosen investment strategy.

In the long run, the greatest profit can be obtained from a simple strategy. It is enough to buy stocks and keep them as long as possible until their value goes up.

In fact, securities of reliable issuers are rarely cheaper. Even economic crises are not as scary for them as they are for bank deposits.

5. Stock valuation

Experts do not recommend evaluating the value of the investment portfolio too often. If you break this rule, there is a great risk of acting out of emotions and selling reasonably priced stocks at a low value.

Nevertheless, you should not forget about evaluating your investments for a long time. Breaking this rule, there is a big risk to miss out on something important.

Developing the strategy and the portfolio criteria evaluation are also significant for a successful investment.

These actions must be performed before the investments are made.

If you don't have time and knowledge for it, it makes sense to benefit from the services of the financial advisors. For a fee, they will show when and which shares to buy and sell.

USEFUL INVESTMENT TIPS FOR BEGINNERS

1. Get help from brokerage companies

Doing investing stuff without brokerage companies, particularly for novice investors, is practically impossible. Frequently, such companies offer assistance in the capacity of advisors to their main services.

The robust brokerage company provides a significant backup for their customers:

- Provides the investors with information about the course of a trading session in the market;

- Formalizes different references;

- Acts as a tax agent for its clients;

- Transfers funds to the investor's personal account in case of sale of shares.

You should follow several rules to choose a reliable partner:

1. There is no need in chasing after minimum commission levels;

2. Before signing the contract, find out unclear issues with the company representative (if they have some);

3. Choose the brokerage company that has a simple and clear work algorithm;

4. Make sure that the software provided by the brokerage company aligns with the client platform.

2. Regularly monitor the market situation

An important component of success in investing capital inequities is knowing the current situation of the market situation.

Realize that you cannot buy securities and, then, just forget about them. You will have to analyze the financial result of the agreement from time to time, as well as invest in the most promising areas.

3. Spend some of your investment in buying stocks directly from issuers

Some issuers spread their shares without the help of the brokers and exchanges. Anyone has the right to buy such securities directly from the company. You can find similar offers on the Internet, along with suggestions to contact the organization that issued the investor of interest to the stock.

Keep in mind that there is a rather high level of risk when buying stocks directly from the issuers. In most cases, new companies sell securities in this way. The probability of their failure is much higher. However, if you are quite lucky, this option can bring a much higher income.

When buying shares directly from the issuers, you can get a discount. Often, companies low the price by almost 5% in case of purchase by a pre-determined amount.

4. Buy shares of the issuers with few competitors

Investing in securities, choose the companies that are the leaders or monopolists in their field of activity.

You better not buy securities of the issuers whose income is determined by season or fashion.

It is difficult to predict the future of trading companies. Today, they could have a huge demand and earn big profits. But after the glut of the market, the sales slow down substantially so that the profits decline ↓. Such offers must be avoided.

5. Focus on long-term investments in stocks

To make the profit more tangible, shares should be held for several years. It makes no sense to sell securities right after there are some changes in the market. A better solution is to wait for periods of stability.

The maximum profit can be obtained by those who can wait for a longer time. It should not be forgotten that, in the long run, the market always has an upward trend.

INVESTMENT PRINCIPLES
OF WARREN BUFFET

Warren Buffet is an American billionaire who made a fortune on successful investments. He is considered to be one of the most successful investors in history, using own investment rules for investing the capital.

Forming an investment portfolio and searching for profitable assets, Buffett methodically analyzes companies according to the following parameters: Simplicity and clarity of business;

- Stability and reputation of the company;

- Availability of the development prospects;

- Competence and honesty of top managers;

- Rational distribution of profit;

- Providing shareholders with transparent information about the state of the business and its profitability;

- The profitability of activity;

- The ratio of the market business value increase to the increase in the retained earnings;

- Profit margin;

- If the price of stocks is overestimated or underestimated in comparison with its real value.

So, analyzing the market business value and securities of the company, Buffet conducts if all the aspects of the business are advantageous for him as an investor.

Various methods for evaluating the efficiency of commercial activities are applied. If data is open, you can analyze financial stability and the likelihood of bankruptcy.

Successful investors recommend studying the news content and find for undervalued stocks (securities, which market value is lower than the nominal value).

The main investment rules by Warren Buffet

1. **You need to buy shares when their market value is significantly lower than the actual price**. The best option is buying securities which value does not exceed 2/3 of the price of the net assets (when converted to 1 share).

2. **Be patient.** The mandatory investors don't expect an instant profit. The one who is willing to get rich is unlikely to get rich.

3. **You have to work out the moderation and discipline**. You don't have to give in to panic by buying or selling assets when there is the smallest volatility on the market.

4. **Select companies the activity of which is clear to you.** Realizing key business processes, the opportunities for their optimization and getting the maximal benefit of the activity, the investor becomes one of the business owners, not just a shareholder.

5. **Long-term prospects are more profitable than short-term ones**. It is necessary to choose the shares of the companies with assessing their activity for 4-5 years in advance. To choose securities that will generate income for a long time, give preference to companies whose products are in constantly high demand and which product prices are not regulated by the state.

6. **Choosing a company to invest in, pay attention to the honesty and competence of its managers.** If the manager aims at increasing the profits for the shareholders and knows how to increase the value of the business – it is a big perk. You better not trust the firms that confidently guarantee some income, as well as those for which accounting is poorly established or non-transparent.

7. **Risk diversification allows receiving profit in a long-term prospect.** If you are thinking about where to start, create an investment portfolio of stocks of companies with different levels of profitability. So, you are more likely to get money. You must also understand that it's okay to get the money in 6 out of ten companies.

HOW TO IDENTIFY THE STOCK THAT IS ABOUT TO GROW?

What is stock growth?

When a company grows in size, it can frequently receive bigger profits. And these bigger profits might lead to raising the stocks in price.

Most commonly, the stocks of the fast-growing companies grow rapidly.

Frequently, these are newer companies that have created some innovative production or found the modern ways of selling old production.

Maybe, they have made up new technology, or, maybe, they have worked out a smart way on how to sell conventional products in the untapped market.

Why the trading of a growth stock is a good idea?

Imagine you have finally created your trading account and accumulated the part of the capital intended for the trade. So, now, you are looking for the best way to boost this capital.

Do you face a lack of options? Well, you can buy the shares of blue chips such as Ford, General Electric or Coca Cola. These companies are reputable and have a quite solid history, and will probably be around for some time. Likely, you will receive dividends because such companies grow slowly but steadily.

By the way, possibly, these companies will face rapid growth, for example, 50-100% or more per year.

If you are a short-term trader, who trades during the day, or holds stocks for weeks, stock growth can bring you some exciting news. This can result in volatile pricing and amazing trading settings.

In a nutshell, stock growth is about following the trends and trying to grow your capital at the fastest rate.

WHAT ARE THE REASONS FOR STOCK GROWTH?

What is driving a company's stocks to grow? What makes a company grow?

Companies are always involved in the business to raise permanent revenue. They provide services for people, sell goods.

For example, Amazon. The company was established at the end of the 90s as an online bookstore, at the time when internet shopping was just beginning to become popular. For the time being, it has become a large infrastructure that allows anyone to buy things online.

Another example is Coca Cola. This company developed a formula of soda beverages, being loved and bought by people all over the world. The company has become one of the biggest world companies trading its drinks throughout the planet.

Both examples show the companies having success in producing products or services needed by a lot of people or businesses because of having found an ideal way to supply it.

But it is worth mentioning that the stock growth can happen not only to Amazon, Coca Cola, or other innovative companies that always offer and develop something new and popular. Actually, these could be developing companies or small companies selling old production in a renewed way.

An insurance company can reap a benefit from new legislation, obliging to buy a certain kind of insurance. The firm rapidly jumps to find as many clients as possible. Also, it can be the business that uses new untapped technology in order to attract potential clients, for example, selling them on Facebook or Instagram.

This is an approximate overview of how and why a company can grow up. It's also relevant to note that the stock price can rise without the company's factor.

Stock prices might reflect what the market predicts for the company. You may find stocks of a turbulent price even if a company doesn't bring any big money. But since the market believes in its successful future, the company could reach the stage when the profits kick off flowing.

How to identify stock growth?

Currently, you may be thrilled to dive into fast-growing companies, to invest or trade.

Search and name for growing names require a lot of knowledge and endeavor. So, here is a list of pointers to help you get started.

☑ Seek for gripping metrics and fundamental stories

The basics of the company are everything relevant to the company: what provokes its sales, financial resources and profits.

Stock growth can frequently be placed with fascinating fundamental stories. They can be leaders in their market niche or extremely competitive firms in their industry. They can give advantages to basic externalities. For example, economic or social changes, new legislation, or a new governance team, oriented on expansion.

From studying underlying indicators, good things, which should be taken into consideration, are the increase in the number of earnings and the sequence of this increase. This is usually depicted in the EPS metric.

Also, take into account that seeking growth names, you can often come across the stocks with high P/E (price/earnings) ratio. This might happen because the market anticipates the profit to be much higher in the short-run (as the company grows) so that the investors seem willing to pay higher stock sums.

☑ Search for trendy stocks moving upward

At the end of the day, the price is paid off in the market. If you are willing to grow the capital instantly, you ought to possess stocks increasing in price.

So, look for the stocks that permanently trend up in with bigger lows. You may take advantage of momentum technical indicators such as sliding averages, used as filters helping you find those stocks.

Actually, uptrends are not the sole things to seek for. You can also search for stocks that fall out of the trading range or stay at high trading volume. This might signal that the market is excited about future stocks.

☑ Assess the social triggers

Social amendments may contribute to growth in many companies and branches. Let's come back to the middle of the 90s. If you had been the investor anticipating the e-commerce boom on the Internet, you could have made some investments in Amazon.

Or, for example, if, in the 2000s, you had foreseen a global social-media obsession, you could have bought shares of Facebook or Twitter.

Such kinds of insightful observations can inform you about a wonderful tempo of stock growth. So, strive to keep track of the growing needs and lifestyle changes in modern society.

Try to make it kind of an exercise in order to spot what people are interested in.

How StockstoTrade can help you to track down and trade with stock growth?

Maybe, you are glad to go after these growing companies. But you are hesitating where and how to start?

The next action is to set yourself on the opportunity to find and explore fascinating stocks easily. Such stocks demonstrate the potential for future growth.

The **StocksToTrade** is created solely for this purpose.

StocksToTrade is a painstakingly built platform. It is a trade and research platform created to assist individual traders to find and trade with best stocks.

The platform could help you solve all the trading needs. If you are concentrated on stock growth, familiarize with these features thoroughly:

- **An all-seeing news scanner** looks for high and low SEC filings, news stories, and even social media mentions of your favorite stocks. You can simply set the platform to monitor your stocks so that you will be kept informed about any buzz or hype straight away.

- **A powerful stock screener** allows scanning all types of trading criteria as frameworks such as EPS or P/E ratios or favorite templates of high-potential diagram patterns. Pressing several buttons, you will provoke the screener to deliver the whole list of all the stocks that corresponding to a certain criterion.

- **Elegant charting capabilities** help increase the technical indicators, the price fluctuates and place trading notifications on all of your favorite stocks. You are able to look through what's presently going on with each stock quickly.

The conclusion

Trading or investing only in fast-growing names can be tempting and potentially advantageous but you should know what you are doing and what are you keeping track of.

Make time to completely digest aforesaid advantages about how to spot stock growth. They might seem simple, although you better follow, make considered decisions, and keep things easy.

To sum up, make sure you use the finest tools that will help you cut down the curve of the studying and master how to define the forward-looking names. **StocksToTrade** will help you.

MOMENTUM TRADING

HOW TO TRACK DOWN TOP PERFORMING STOCKS

Momentum trading is known as the action of pursuing high-effective stocks, buying and striving to sell stocks. Momentum stocks are stocks with long-term growth, typically during a period from three to 12 months, with permanently high returns over the same period.

The theory that lies in the base of momentum trading stocks differs from the regulation of the trade value and growth of shares. Value stocks are identified by searching for stocks ongoing costs of which exceed their present prices, while growth stocks are those for which the present price doesn't mirror the future value.

For both value and growth stocks the objective value of the company, which is performed by stock, is necessary to determine the price to buy. On the other hand, the value is irrelevant for momentum stocks - the stock value will keep on growing according to its current tendency at least in a short-term prospect.

Momentum trading has historically exceeded value-based trading until the uptrend proceeds. For instance, let's take the technological boom of the 1990s. At that time, the technology stocks exceeded the market dramatically until the momentum fell. Nevertheless, momentum trading needs the short-term because it needs frequent mobile capital from stocks, the momentum of which infiltrates to those that are about to heat up. Therefore, momentum trading includes placing a much bigger number of trades than value-based trading, which may lead to additional trading fees and be disadvantageous from a tax standpoint.

Usually, the momentum stocks work best when the market wholly pushes to new highs. In this case, the investor's moods tend to be optimistic and numerous stocks set permanent growth. On the other hand, when the market approaches its bottom, the value stocks are the best for trading. Despite the momentum stocks that may exist, they will be rarely met through the bear market, and a lot of reliable stocks will be likely underestimated concerning their objective value.

Momentum Stock Criteria

The very first step in momentum trading is the identification of impulse shares in the wider market. There exist several clear criteria that can be used either in combination or separately to narrow down the stocks in trend. The best way to apply these criteria is via the stock scanner that will return a small list of potential momentum, which might additionally be analyzed before the trading.

Earnings growth

One of the most common features of momentum trading is that it permanently informs about the growing earnings-per-share and revenue. As a rule, a lot of momentum stocks, releasing earnings reports, also outperform the analyst predictions. To track down stocks with accelerating earnings, scan for stocks, whose earnings increased in a quarter-over-quarter for the last year and were bigger than the same previous period.

High returns

Because the momentum stocks apt to outperform the market in a short-term prospect, there is a simple method to define the potential momentum stocks. It is scanning for the existing stocks that bring bigger than S&P 500 or any other index earnings for the last 6 months or 1 year.

Scanning of the first pass will likely give a lot of stocks, which later can be narrowed down by deleting the bottom 10% repeatedly until the list is brief enough for the further research of each stock.

Assertive Short-Term Averages

When the stock gradually grows up its short-term moving averages of price, it should exceed its long-term moving price averages. Thereby, the momentum stocks can be identified via scanning for average indicators made up according to their timeframe. In practical terms, it can mean the search of stocks where the 10-day sliding average is higher than the sliding average for 50 days and, for its part, surpasses the 100-day sliding average.

Setting new peaks

Another result of subsequent growing tendency, typical for momentum stocks, lies down in setting new highs to break those highs by moving higher. The pivotal fact is that the determination of how your trading plan conforms to a high period. For instance, for daily trading, the momentum stocks, which consistently break their 4-day highs, are more suitable goals for momentum trading than the stocks breaking their 20- or 55-day highs.

The conclusion

Momentum trading can turn out to be pretty risky as it is rarely clear for how long the momentum stocks will go on. A smart choice for you to enter into a position is critical because the slowing down of the momentum may destroy your momentum trade rapidly, and the reversal might be serious if the stock is considered to be overvalued at the end of its growth. Looking for the momentum trades, it is better to set the positions in stocks whose momentum is only ripening, not those whose momentum grows older. As a rule, it is better not to maintain stocks overnight as soon as momentum reduces.

However, using a broader trading plan your momentum trade may become an advantageous and sustainable strategy. The example is to use the momentum as a factor for the delimitation of stock value for investing or for determining the points of entry and exit for the value stock. Besides, the momentum can be used as a short-term strategy in a wider context of a long-term strategy based on the value. However, if you made up your mind to apply the momentum trading, it is important to realize the difference between investments established on the momentum and value, as well as have the ability to identify the stocks having the momentum.

PASSIVE INCOME

Passive income - is the income that you generate independently while working or being out of work. In fact, it is a way of earning money with the help of a ready product that brings income under minimal control by an owner's side.

Passive income is the result of previously invested money, effort and time. It is work on the prospect - sometimes you should sweat blood for 1 or 2 years before the project pays off and becomes profitable.

Let's say, working for a chief, you distribute your effort equally and receive small money for small responsibilities. And if you are willing to have a passive income, firstly, you invest in it your funds, intellect, experience and time. Only then you will be able to get a successful result. All risks are yours – a success is one hundred percent yours as well as a failure. So a myth, saying passive income is a kind of job consisting of just lying around and getting money for this – is wrong.

Almost all the articles devoted to passive income colorfully describe what a great money you could earn without a need of doing something. You know, people, who write such things, will either not grind anything in such a business, or are going to sell you some scheme of passive earnings. In reality, this scheme, of course, will not work for you but for your hosts.

To receive this money, you should find the sources of passive income, and there is a bunch of ways. Everything depends on your character and how much time efforts and time you are ready to devote to it.

When someone is looking for an opportunity to earn additional income, they are usually advised to find a temporary part-time job. But what to do if you don't have either time or energy for it? In this case, you will need to find the other ways to get passive income – earning money with few investments of time and effort.

Here are 20 ways for you to earn passive income:

1. Try partner marketing and start selling

This passive income approach is more appropriate for blogs and active websites. You can start promoting any products on your website and receive a fixed fee or percentage of the sales. It is not difficult to make money in such a way as it could seem at a first sight since many companies are interested in promoting their products through as many places as possible.

To find the partnership offers, you can address directly to producers or on profile sites. Best of all, the situation when the advertised product or service is interesting for you or/ and matches the theme of the website.

2. Try index funds

Index funds make it possible to receive income from investments in the stock market absolutely passively. For instance, if you invest in a fund based on S&P 500, the funds will be invested in the common market, and you won't have to think about how to manage your capital and whether sell or buy shares of certain companies. All these points will be managed by the fund, which forms its investment portfolio depending on the state of a particular index.

You can also choose a fund working with any index. There exist funds taking up different business industries –

energetics, precious metals, banking, developing markets, and others. The only thing that remained for you is to decide what you want to take up and then invest money and repose. From this moment, your stock portfolio will be working on autopilot.

3. Make videos for YouTube

This is quite fast-developing area for the time being. You can make videos for absolutely any category: music, tutorials, comedies, film reviews – just everything, and then upload them on YouTube. After that, you can connect Google AdSense to these videos and they'll automatically display ads. When viewers click on this ad, you'll receive money from Google AdSense.

Your main task is to create worthy videos, promote them on social sites and maintain a sufficient number of them to secure income from several clips. It's not so easy to shoot and edit the video, but, later, you will be able to receive passive money from this extra source.

4. Write an e-book

Of course, this can be a rather time-consuming process. Nevertheless, when you write a book and place it on some trading platforms, it can provide you with income for years. You can sell the book on your own site or enter into a partnership agreement with other sites that are relevant to the book topic.

5. Make your photos to bring money online

Are you fond of taking photos? If so, then you have all the chances to turn it into a passive income source. Photobanks like Shutterstock and iStockphoto can provide you with platforms for selling your snapshots. You will receive a percentage or fixed rate for each photography sold to the site customer.

In this case, each picture represents its separate source of income, which can work over and over. You just need to make a portfolio, upload it on one or several platforms and, now, your actions are finished there. All technical issues, concerning selling photos, are solved by means of the web platform.

6. Buy high-yield stocks

Having created a portfolio of high-yield stocks, you might get a source of regular income with an annual percentage rate significantly exceeding the interests of bank deposits.

You mustn't forget that the high-yield stocks-are the same stocks, so you have to always overestimate capital. Consequently, you will make a profit from several sources: from dividends and income from the invested capital. You also should buy such stocks and fill out appropriate forms to create a brokerage account.

7. Write a real book and receive an author's fee

In this way, you will have to take pains. But when the work is finished and the book will be in stock, it becomes another source of passive income.

This is especially true when you manage to sell a book to a publisher who is willing to pay you a sales fee. You will receive a percentage from each sold copy, and if the book is popular, this percentage can result in substantial amounts of money. In addition, these payments can last for years.

Mike Piper from ObviousInvestor.com has recently done that. He had written the book, «Investing in Simple Language», which was only sold on Amazon. The first book had become so profitable that he decided to create the whole series, resulting in the books bringing him a total of six figures annually.

8. Get cashback from transactions with credit cards

Many credit cards provide cashback in the size of 1-5% from the total amount of purchase. Anyway, you go on shopping sprees and spend money there, don't you?

Such perks allow providing yourself with so-called passive income in the form of reducing expenses out of the actions that you still fulfill.

9. Sell your handmade goods online

In this area, the possibilities are unlimited: you can sell almost any goods or services. It can be something you have created and made with your own hands, or it can be a digital product (programs, DVDs or training videos).

For trading, you can use the profile resource if you suddenly do not have your own website or blog. In addition, you can enter into a partnership agreement by offering the product to sites of relevant topics or using platforms like Click Bank.

You can learn how to sell goods on the Internet and earn sufficiently on this. Maybe this is not a completely passive income, but it is certainly more passive than the usual work that you have to go every morning.

10. Make investments in a real estate

This way falls into a category of semi-passive income because estate investments imply, at least, small activity. Nevertheless, if you have an estate that you are already renting out, you only have to maintain its condition.

Besides, there exist professional property managers who can manage your property for a commission of approximately 10% of the rent. Such professional managers help to make the process of making a profit more passive, at the same time taking the part of it.

One more way to invest in real estate is to pay back a loan. If you take out a loan to purchase the premises that you will lease, each month, your tenants will gradually pay off this debt. When the full amount is paid, your profit will increase sharply, and your relatively small investment will turn into a full-fledged program.

11. Create a selling website

If there is a product that you know the ropes about, you can kick off its realization on a profile site. The methodology is the same as the one when selling a product of your own manufacture, except that you do not have to deal with the production itself.

After some time, you may find that you can add similar products. If this happens, the website will start to generate substantial profits.

If you find a way to deliver goods directly from the manufacturer to a buyer, you won't even have to get your hands dirty. Maybe, this is not completely passive income, but it is very close to it.

12. Make investments in investment trusts of estate property (REIT)

For example, you decided to invest money in the estate but you don't want to spend much time on it. Then, the investment trusts will help you as they represent something like a fund that owns different projects in the estate property area. The funds are managed by specialists, so, you won't need to put your finger in their work.

One of the pivotal perks of investments in REIT-trusts is that, usually, they bring in much higher dividends than stocks, bonds, and bank deposits. In addition, you can also sell your share in trust anytime. This makes your assets more liquid than independent estate management.

13. Buy a blog

Every year thousands of blogs are created and, after a while, some of them end up abandoned. If you can buy a blog with a sufficient amount of visitors (and so with sufficient money flow), it can become an excellent source of your passive income.

Most blogs use Google AdSense, which pays for the ads placed on the website once a month. Partnership arrangements can also be made to provide additional income. Both of these profit streams will be yours if you possess a blog.

From a financial point of view, blogs typically sell for up to 24 times the monthly income this blog can generate. It means if the site can earn $250 per month, most likely, you could buy it for $ 3000. Subsequently, investing $ 3,000, you can receive $ 1,500 annually. Probably, you will manage to buy a site for a less amount of money if the owner is willing to get rid of this asset. On some sites, there are some «eternal» materials that won't lose its topicality and will bring income for years after the publication.

Bonus tip: If you buy such a website and fill it with some fresh content, you will be capable of increasing your monthly income and, after a while, you will be able to sell the site again at a significantly higher price than you had bought.

At last, instead of buying the blog, set up your own one as this is also a good way to make money.

14. Become a passive income partner

Do you know a company that needs some capital for extending the business? If so, you can become a short-term angel and provide this capital. Ask for a share of stocks instead of giving a loan to the company's owner. In this case, the company's owner will run the work of the company while you are a passive partner participating in the business.

15. Rent non-residential apartment on Airbnb

The Airbnb concept appeared about just a few years ago, but quickly took the world's popularity like a storm. Airbnb allows people to travel around the world and pay much less for accommodation than in usual hotels. By taking part in Airbnb, you can use your house to accommodate guests and earn extra money only by renting.

The amount of income will depend on the size and condition of your apartment, its location. Naturally, if your house is located in an expensive city or near a popular resort, the income will be much higher. This is the way to make money from free space in your house, which, in any case, would be free for someone else.

16. Develop your online courses

Every person is an expert in some areas. Why don't you create an online course connected to your hobby? There are several ways to create and conduct online courses. One of the easiest ways is to use websites like Udemy. com. With over 8 million students, Udemy is a great way to present your content to others.

After having created the online course, it can work for you when you sleep. What will you include in your course? You can add video-tutorial lessons, checklists to fulfill the recommended steps in steps, sell small e-books in addition to the lessons, or audiophiles for people listening while traveling, as well as interviews with experts and like-minded people.

In fact, you can create several packages at different prices. Some people will want everything, so, you can add an all-inclusive segment at the highest price and two cheaper segments to get the maximum order volume.

17. Become a recommendation source

Every small business needs a source of recommendations to maintain sales. Draw up a list of entrepreneurs whose services you use every day and the ones which you can recommend for collaboration. Connect with them and find out if they have a payment system for recommendations.

You can add familiar accountants, electricians, plumbers, landscape designers, carpet cleaners, and anyone else to the list. Be prepared to recommend these services to your friends, relatives, and colleagues. You can receive a commission from every recommendation just by talking to people.

Do not underestimate referral programs in the professional field. If the company you work in has bonuses for recommending new employees or new customers, use them. This is very easy money.

18. Write an app

Applications can be incredibly lucrative revenue streams. Think about how many people today have smartphones.

Yes, almost everyone! People go crazy and can't help downloading loads of apps - and for a good reason.

Applications make people's lives easier. It doesn't matter if it helps to post beautiful pictures or keep track of some tasks - there is always the application that is useful to someone.

19. Create an online management

If you are not into writing articles or making videos but you are willing to earn money on the Internet, try to create interactive management. A good example is the Pat Flyn website of SecurityGuardTrainingHQ.com. The site has a map of the United States, which allows you to click on any of the states to see the requirements for security officers in it.

Providing specific information in a guide format, you can make money using the previously mentioned tools: advertising through Google AdSense, affiliate links, etc. Besides, you can even sell a subscription to your guide.

20. Make money on what your everyday habits

Yes, you can make money on certain things that you already do.

For example, InboxDollars allows you to earn money on playing games, shopping online, searching the Internet, and much more. Swagbucks works according to the same algorithm.

INVESTMENT STRATEGIES

DIRECTIONS, TYPES AND EXAMPLES

A proven investment strategy is the major activity of any trader, which needs many hours of monitoring and analysis. There exist a lot of strategies focused on different styles and ways of investing.

1. What is an investment strategy?

Under the term «strategy» investors understand a certain combination of activities and methods with a view to achieving a set financial outcome, management tactic of personal capital on the market. There is an abundance of defining this term but, in a nutshell, it's possible to say that the **investment strategy** is a clearly described sequence of actions used in certain circumstances on the financial market, aimed at making a profit.

Usually, the strategy implies the restriction of a risk level, conditions under which an asset is acquired or sold, as well as certain borderline values of prices, profit or loss, reaching which intervention in the process is essential. The presence of such conditions is vital for an investor who is willing to generate income from his activity.

The achievement of the desirable results, as well as the level of risk and the duration of the investment, directly depends on the chosen strategy.

18. The significance of determining your investment strategy

Possessing an investment strategy means having a list with instructions that assists you to go through the investment process. This will help you to exclude the potential investments that might have terrible overtime or the ones that don't meet the rules of the investment goals you wish to obtain.

It is important to discover what you want to achieve when creating an investment strategy. It is helpful just to state that you are willing to earn money or to become a wealthy person. A much better target is to say: "I want to reach an 8% average annual return from my investment risks during the following 15 years in order to gather $ 300 000, which are going to be used for buying a cottage house. A considered and visualized goal is better because the investment strategy is useless without its proper understanding. There exists DIY.FUND to help you work out a portfolio and control the investments for a better understanding of how to deal with them.

The main types of investing strategies:

1. Growth investing

It is the investment strategy tailored to capital growth. The investors are looking for companies that demonstrate signs of above-average growth via revenues and profits, even if the stock price is high from the perspective of such metrics like price-to-earnings or price-to-book ratios. Peter Lynch made a major contribution to growth investing. However, it is a relatively risky investment strategy in growth.

2. Value investing

It is the investment strategy that became famous by Warren Buffet.

According to the investment theory, it is clear and easy: buy stocks cheaper than they should be. Tracking down for stocks that are undervalued requires a lot of fundamental analysis of underlying companies. As soon as you find them, their price takes a lot of time to form. This acquisition and system require a cautious investor only in case of a right-made call. At least, all the investors must be aware of essential investment basics.

2. Small-Cap Investing

This is a tactic that is suitable for investors who want to take more risk in their portfolios. As we can see it from the term, small-cap investing entails buying up stocks in smaller firms with a lower market capitalization (usually between $200 million and $1 billion). Usually, small stocks attract investors because of its ability to remain unnoticed. Meanwhile, big-cap stocks will be always overvalued because they are in the center of the attention of the majority. Small-cap stocks are apt to have less attention on them because:

■ Investors keep off the risks;

■ Institutional investors (like mutual funds) are constrained when it comes to investing in small-cap firms.

Only seasoned fund investors ought to use small-cap investing as they appear to be more changeable and, thereby, hard to trade.

4. Income Investing

An excellent way to accumulate wealth over the years is investing our income, which envisages buying of securities that payout the returns on a daily basis. Bonds are the most common way to provide fixed-income security. Also, these are stocks that pay off the dividend-paying stocks, mutual funds, exchange-traded funds (ETFs), and real estate investment trusts (REITs). Fixed income investments supply a robust stream with minimal risk and, depending on it, the investor might be willing to take over and embrace at least a small part of every investment strategy.

5. Socially Responsible Investing

It is a portfolio focused on social and environmentally-friendly companies that are competitive depending on other kinds of securities in a typical market environment. In our present industrial world, the general public and investors anticipate companies to sustain some social conscience and invest their money where their mouths are. The SRI is one of the ways to search for returns that pose considerable collateral benefits for everyone.

How to choose the right investment strategy? The main recommendations.

There is a number of recommendations regarding the choice of investment strategies, following which can help novice traders choose and master the trading option that is right for them.

- **A personal strategy.** At first, most investors work according to one of the well-known strategies. Nevertheless, as you gain experience and identify your own trading characteristics, it's worth adjusting it to your style, adding new rules, changing correlation, achieving optimal efficiency of its use.

- **The timing.** You should not strive to use complicated strategies requiring a lot of time if the latter is limited. It often happens that a selected trading method can't be combined with another activity according to some important reasons. For instance, a working day correlates with a period of increasing or decreasing market volatility. In this case, you should make sufficient time to detriment of the other occupations or refuse such a strategy, and choose a more appropriate one.

- **Risk control.** Aggressive strategies look attractive because of the high potential profit, though, firstly, you must answer the question whether your skills are sufficient for such trading, and also whether you can afford to lose all the invested funds in the future. If the answer is no, it is better to choose less risky trading options.

- **The amount of capital.** Different strategies require various sizes of initial investments and also «airbags» from free funds. You should never "pull up" a strategy for a deposit if it is not enough. It is a better idea to choose another one, a more suitable trading option for yourself.

- **Psychological features**. There exist a bunch of interesting strategies, although not all of them will be suitable for a particular person. If it is obvious that a person has a lack of patience, he better not hopes that while choosing the strategy with a large amount of analysis such a feature will disappear. If the trader is too nervous and emotional, it is better for him to refuse using trading ways associated with a big number of restrictions and strict discipline. The best is to choose a strategy that is appropriate to the character of a particular investor.

Following these rules don't ensure the profit. However, we can say that it can significantly cut the trader's challenging path towards choosing the trading method that suits him the best.

The conclusion

There are a lot of investment strategies so that any investor can choose the most suitable for him. When determining the optimal for oneself, take into consideration not only its profitability but also comparability with own capabilities and psychological characteristics.

HOW TO SAVE MONEY? TOP 5 TIPS CONCERNING FINANCE MANAGEMENT.

We have made a selection of tips from leading experts on financial planning of large foreign companies. These are simple but effective recommendations which help to treat your money in more reasonable way in 2020.

TIP No1. Work hard and save up more part of your income.

Everybody knows that at least 10% of your total income should be saved up. But what if you cut down on spending money and try to save most of the funds? That's exactly what Renee Kwok advises to do. Renee Kwok is a certificated expert on financial planning and general director TFC Financial (Asset Management Company in Boston worth $1mlrd.)

In addition, Kwok recommend investing money. When savings are kept in the drawer of the table they won't bring additional benefit in the form of interest, although they could.

Even if you are not ready to take risks, an ordinary deposit in a bank with a minimal rate will help to protect your funds from inflation and cash on it a bit.

TIP No2. First and foremost- sort out with your debts.

Debt is not a verdict but it can adversely influence on your financial goals. In order to help people balance their debt payments, SoFi Company designed 3-step method. Loren

Anastasia, certificated specialist on financial planning, named it fireball method. Firstly, you should pay out a loan with the highest percentage rate. The maximum amount of money should be directed towards its repayment, while not forgetting about the gradual repayment of less problematic debts.

After, when the problematic debt has finally paid out, an expert advises to direct as much money as possible on saving even if you have some unredeemed loans with low rate. Such strategy will help to create so-called safety cushion or save up a sufficient sum of money on a big purchase, for example: a flat or a car.

When you have enough savings in order to feel confident in the future, you can focus on a final repayment of all left loans.

TIP No3. Save up money on different goals

Luis Rosa, a certificated specialist on financial planning from the company Build a Better Financial Future. He suggests distributing funds, left after all necessary expenses, into several accumulation categories: funds for a vacation, wedding or for making your living. Ideally, if these are not cash envelopes, but high-yield savings accounts in different banks. An expert considers that saving process on a defined goal increases the motivation. You can observe what the part of your salary is spent on and how close this or that target is.

TIP No4. Avoid living beyond your means

One of the most common financial advice of our time is to live worse than you can afford. And there are good reasons for this. After all, spending all your money on daily needs, you will not advance in achieving long-term goals.

This is a really easy trap to fall into if you try to trying to keep up with friends who spend a lot, or themselves began to earn more. So try to make your permanent income stay relatively reasonable and sustained. And the remaining funds should be put aside long-term goal or invested. This advice was shared by Katie Brewer, a certified financial planner and founder of Your Richest Life.

TIP No5.Insure your life right now

If your relatives are dependent on your income, experts advise to insure your life. In case of emergency and unpredictable situations they will be able to proceed their normal existence or pay off the debts.

This category also includes health and home insurance. It will save large amounts in case of illness or emergency.

HOW TO REACH FINANCIAL FREEDOM AND BECOME FINANCIALLY INDEPENDENT?

What is financial independence?

Financial independence - is the threshold beyond which there are many prospects and opportunities. It is the overriding goal to which you must strive to get rid of all your monetary obligations and become independent of money, subjugate them.

Financial independence is what a prudent person strives for, rather than just dreaming. It involves taking deliberate steps towards achieving this goal, not engaging in excuses: «I will start tomorrow» or «I am not a financier».

The second large problem you can face with on the way to your financial independence is banal laziness because you realize that you will have to read a lot of finance literature, make some steps, seek for additional income sources, learn how to refuse yourself and take a bunch of steps yet.

Strangely enough but your laziness can also be the impetus for financial independence. Let's draw a simple analogy: laziness is the engine of progress because if it were not for this particular feature of human nature, we would not have cars, food processors and all that can significantly reduce the time to work and take any actions.

The same applies to financial independence: the earlier you decide about your way to achieving your goal, the sooner you start enjoying a permanent rest and doing nothing-your money will do it instead of you.

So, financial independence can be reached in that case if you have multiple sources of passive income that make money in your life and you may not be able to work. But before you search for these sources, you need to take the following steps:

- Learn how to dispose rationally of the funds that you have at the moment. You must understand one simple rule: only reasonable economy and cost optimization will be able to provide a stable financial position according to which all your further steps towards gaining financial independence will depend. Make up your financial plan to make sure that your monthly expenses do not exceed the totality of your income. Secure yourself against different kinds of surprises (finance airbag, medical protection); get rid of all debts and credits. The economy must be reasonable. You shouldn't restrict yourself in everything. When you start to implement your plan you will see how easily you can spend money without limiting yourself and always staying in the win, that is, your cash will always stay stable and assets and accumulations will grow.

- After having made your financial plan and started following it, it is necessary to take care of your «golden stock». It implies opening a deposit in a bank that every month you will top up and then obtain interests from it. It is better when capitalization interests join to deposit and then interests are accrued on interests.

- You must understand that by depositing 10% of your income, you can save 100% of your salary on a deposit, which is a minimum requirement for financial independence, except for 60-80 years. Most likely, this option will not suit you, so you must constantly upgrade your skill in making money and increase the size of your income. You also need to invest in yourself, in the skills of managing your finances effectively, in exploring new opportunities to raise money. Only this approach will allow you to accelerate your movement to the desired financial independence.

Only having a great desire, pursuit, and implementation of all the necessary steps will you be able to say in a few years that you are independent of finances and now they work for you and you - have a rest.

SECURED FINANCIAL FUTURE

In modern times, many people live only for today. Owing to various circumstances, strategic planning and secured financial future get the low priorities resulting in variable objective reactions on a similar tendency.

On the one hand, it is significantly important to enjoy every moment of our life, live here and now, and focus on the events going on at the moment.

And for many of us, this approach is one of the best ways to feel the taste of life, enjoy the present, and not to become attached to the problems and tasks that may appear later.

On the other hand, ignoring sober views of the future is pure irresponsibility. The modern world is so unpredictable that abrupt change of circumstances can catch a person off guard. And if there is no adequate reaction to the changes, then a very deplorable situation can develop. That is why it makes sense to plan everything in a few steps forward and pay a little attention to the longer-term prospects.

Secured financial future, what can be done now?

The history of world development has clearly shown that people with sufficient funds have the best adaptation to changes. The presence of financial resources turns any stressful situation in a favorable environment. There is an indisputable fact that the upper class, in whose hands impressive capital has been always concentrated, calmly survived wars, disasters, and natural disasters.

For the time being, there is no need in being a direct descendant of count blood in order to secure your future. If previously rich people were either born or became through unthinkable efforts, now obtaining the necessary benefits lies in the zone of accessibility of any person. That is, your chances for a brighter future are greater than ever.

What options can secure your well financial future and worthy senility?

- Firstly, it is money accumulation. A capital formation is your financial safety cushion for all the cases.

- Secondly, these are your financial goals.

Here are 5 categories of financial goals for you to set:

1. Save the standards of living and upgrade them in the future;

2. Provide higher education for children, i.e. foresee the funds for this purpose;

3. Ensure financial security (protection) of the family;

4. Create personal capital, gain financial freedom;

5. Transfer capital, assets to children and grandchildren; create the inheritance for future generations.

- Thirdly, these are, of course, your investments. Your funds must work. Having built the right investment politics, you will be able to provide yourself with passive income for years. This will allow you to make minimal efforts to generate maximum income.

The question of how to secure your financial future concerns everyone. No matter if you are a beginner or professional entrepreneur - you work for money. The only sure way to solve the five above-mentioned universal financial problems (according to your personal financial

---

plan) is to invest carefully and progressively in some reliable global instruments.

EXCHANGE-TRADED FUNDS (ETF)

Exchange-Traded Funds or ETF- these are investment funds the stocks of which are traded on a stock exchange. ETF funds became extremely popular and widely used in the last decade.

In simple terms, ETF is a stocks basket that is an investment fund that keeps track of index meaning and is traded as one security. Stocks price growth of an investment fund indicates on its success and prospect. Funds can't deal with stocks acquisition and other stock exchange assets by themselves.

Most often, they completely copy the composition of stock indices, for example, the PowerShares Fund (QQQ) completely copies the NASDAQ 100 index.

Since the indices themselves are just quantities, not assets, on these quantities the derivatives are created such as futures, options, etc.

Today, almost every stock index has an ETF fund that repeats its structure.

A stock investment fund is a ready-made portfolio of assets that can repeat a specific stock exchange index, or have a portfolio of stocks, or, for example, metals, and other stock goods, that is developed.

Shares of exchange funds are displayed on the stock exchange, like ordinary securities. The most affordable stocks on the market now cost a few cents, the most expensive - hundreds of dollars.

How to buy stocks of ETF

Among the popular brokers that provide the opportunity to buy shares of ETF funds, is the Libertex broker (the minimum deposit for opening an account is 200 USD). To buy stocks, you need to open a trading platform and enter the ticker you are interested in. Coming back to the beginning of the material ETF is a strong financial tool, popular because of its simplicity, flexibility, and essence the stocks of which can bring good returns.

Trading with ETF stocks

You can invest in ETFs using leverage, which significantly reduces collateral requirements. There are pending orders and stop orders in this market. Using these tools, an investor can indicate the price at which he is ready to purchase a particular fund and wait for a counteroffer.

Despite that portfolios are compiled by professionals the damages are possible. For example, if an index starts going down sharply because of the economic situation. In this case, the fund will also fall in cost.

It is important to pay attention to the fact that the cost of funds is determined based on supply and demand. Accordingly, an investor will have an opportunity to buy ETF cheaper (sometimes more expensive) than a net asset value of a fund. But such deviations will be minimal.

Sometimes there are situations when investment funds demonstrate much higher profitability rather than indexes that are the epitome for them (however the major part of funds still follows the index). On the other hand, the profitability may be much lower than that of indices. Such a phenomenon is called tracking error but practically is absent on the market, since the foundation of the funds' various measures has been taken to eliminate errors.

You will make sure that ETF is extremely valuable trading tools, tailored to stock indices and industry groups that are designed to increase the profitability of the game on the market. Funds also work well to diversify your main account and hedge it with short-term stock reversals.

Most **ETFs** are traded with low liquidity (average daily volume). It means that ETF with lower liquidity may show nominal volatility and be traded in a narrow price range of a few cents a day. In turn, this can reduce their attractiveness as for both candidates and for swing trading, since the possibility of making a profit, in this case, is minimal.

Well-known trader Tony Turner recommends using a daily trading volume of 300,000 shares and more for swing **ETF** trading.

Tony Turner uses ETF in 3 cases:

■ As part of index and sector strategies.

■ For diversification

■ For hedging

Types of Types of ETFs:

As was mentioned above, basically ETF follows indexes. The reason for this is the fact that investors tend to buy stocks that are part of a particular index, besides it is a convenient tool of portfolio investments instead of hundreds of stocks, you should buy stocks of one company (ETF)

■ Particularly global indexes within one state are that indexes that penetrate the whole market completely. These include, for example, Russell 3000, NASDAQ Composite.

- Next are the indices that reflect the state in certain sectors of the economy. The main attention is paid to the securities packet of a defined enterprise. Some funds ignore such kinds of indexes and address them to work with commodities.

- Recently, currency indices have also appeared.

- The indices of debt securities. There are at least six such indexes.

It is necessary to understand which indexes are served as a basis to trade with Exchange investment funds. It will help to make the right decision when buying ETF stocks and also to carry out an essential market analysis.

ETF Structure

3 main classes are singled out among ETFs

- Open Index Mutual Funds

- General Investment Trust Funds

- Principal Exchange Trusts

There is a certain difference between first and third. Open Mutual Fund can reinvest incomes that were obtained as a result of working with shares in the package. As for the Trust Fund – it doesn't have an opportunity.

Open Index Funds may give securities in debt. In this case, such a fund may receive a significant profit from securities that are hard to track down on the market.

ETF cost

ETFs have 3 costs:

- Stock cost

- The second one is determined according to the outcomes based on net fund assets

- The third one is intraday and is calculated based on the value of net assets during the day

It is important to understand that not all exchange-traded investment funds are inherent in high liquidity.

Strategies for working with ETFs

There are several interesting types of strategies that may be used for working with exchange-traded funds. For example, one of them-is well-known diversification. When buying stocks of an exchange-traded fund, an investor diversifies his portfolio at the expense of a collected stock package inside the fund. That is, we are talking about buying a portfolio in a portfolio. But this is not the most important and basic system. One of the varieties of diversification in trading is the purchase of several funds.

Smart distribution of assets

There are 2 variants of strategies-passive and active. In the first case, it concerns collecting a portfolio that will represent the strategic balancing of assets. This system works best in the long run.

As for the active strategy, the investor can balance the portfolio so that there are added assets that can give good returns in the short term.

ETF Risk Hedging

Working with exchange-traded funds allows an investor to hedge his risks. For example, if an investor is afraid of falls on the markets he may buy an inverse exchange-traded fund. Such assets will go up when markets go down.

If investor fears inflation he may invest in bond funds that are protected against price growth. Regarding the currency market, investors have an opportunity to insure them with the help of currency funds. There are such options on ETF that may be used in numerous strategies.

In case of financial troubles or a fall in the crisis, ETFs invest in real gold, silver, and platinum. Reserves of the American SPDR Gold Shares are 1 301 tons of gold, British Securities Gold Funds - 325.8 tons.

6 THE MOST POPULAR ETFS OF 2020

1. Best international Vanguard FTSE developed markets

If you want to add an international influence to your portfolio, big companies in developed countries tend to offer a better risk balance and return. Developing market funds are seductive but it should be taken into consideration that they are significantly risky rather than investments in developed markets.

VEA keeps track of the index designed by FTSE All Cap ex-US. It means that it monitors the companies of any size in advanced companies besides the USA. This investment adds shares in Europe, Canada, and Pacific countries into your portfolio easily. The fund charges a low 0,050% expense ratio.

2. Best for NASDAQ Large-Cap Stocks: Invesco QQQ (QQQ)

The symbol of a ticker QQQ gives an ETF that monitors this NASDAQ 100 index. The NASDAQ consists of 100 the biggest stocks on the NASDAQ stock exchange market that serves traditionally as a home for many technology companies.

If S&P 500 tracks large -cap stocks across both main USA stock exchanges, this index is restricted to just the NASDAQ because you can anticipate your investments to be more strongly influenced by large news in the technology sector more than other industries. This ETF charges 0, 20% expense ratio.

---

3. The best for gold SPDR Gold Trust (GLD)

If you want to invest your funds in gold without visiting jewelers and buying bars of precious metal you're the best option is GLD ETF. GLD is a proxy for prices on a golden bar. It charges 0, 40% ratio.

Gold is also frequently used as a protection from falls on a stock market. When stocks and economics go down, investors often run to gold as an investment safety net. This means that gold frequently trades with inversely to the famous index funds mentioned above- keep in mind that if you decide to convert some of your dollars in GLD.

4. Best for Active Traders: SPDF S&P 500 ETF (SPY)

Yes, S&P is so important that it ranks fourth in this list. It is one of the most widely-traded ETF on the market. As this index tracks the S&P 500 in real -time, active investors use this fund to buy and sell the US stock market in a single trade. SPY was launched in 1993 as the first stock exchange fund.

Active traders give preference to SPY because of its extremely high liquidity. It charges 0, 0945%, expense ratio. But thanks to its fame and trade frequency a lot of investors are willing to put their cash into SPY.

5. Best for Small-Cap Stocks: iShares Russell 2000 ETF (IWM)

Russell 2000 is an index that monitors 2,000 small-cap stocks. It consists of the smallest 2,000 of the Russell 3000 index measured by market capitalization. This index is an excellent way to keep track of the USA market in general but with an accent on smaller firms on public markets instead of the biggest.

IWM charges a 0, 19 expense ratio that is lower than in many mutual funds but far from the bottom ETF industry. Comparatively, with S&P 500 fund, managers of iShares Russell 2000 ETF have four times more stocks for buy and sell to keep index fund in-line with the index.

Some investors claim that smaller shares have more opportunities for growth than big shares while contrarians claim that smaller stocks are more risky and changeable. But if you want to buy a big number of American companies by one click, IWM is a popular way to do it.

6. Best Overall: Vanguard S&P 500 ETF (VOO)

One of the best ETF that comes from the largest mutual fund company: is Vanguard. This ETF monitors the S&P 500 and charges only 0.03% of the expense ratio. Warren Buffett himself even recommended the Vanguard S&P 500 Index Fund by name.

Buying this fund you are exposed to an impact of 500 the largest state companies in the USA. This offers you a great deal of variety with a certain degree of safety net since all investments are concentrated in the US.

Historically, the S&P 500, which in several aspects is a proxy for the United States economy as a whole, returns about 10% a year for a long period. Although past success is not a promise of potential results, and the market may go down at any moment, this index fund is a perfect investment if you have a long-term view.

DISCLAIMER

The opinions and ideas of the author contained in this publication are designed to educate the reader in an informative and helpful manner. While we accept that the instructions will not suit every reader, it is only to be expected that the recipes might not gel with everyone. Use the book responsibly and at your own risk. This work with all its contents, does not guarantee correctness, completion, quality or correctness of the provided information. Always check with your medical practitioner should you be unsure whether to follow a low carb eating plan. Misinformation or misprints cannot be completely eliminated. Human error is real!

Design: NataliaDesign

Picture: bookzv/ www.shutterstock.com

Printed in Great Britain
by Amazon